How to Overcome Your Fears and Excuses to Achieve Your Goals

"Hope is not a strategy."
Chris Voss, author -Never Split the Difference

You are a success because of what you do, not because of what you don't do. It's time to act... put into place and implement the steps to move forward towards achieving your goal.

Sitting around all day waiting and hoping your dreams will come true are futile. It's not enough just to think positive and do visualizations, you must take the necessary steps to turn your dreams into reality.

You will learn:

- To get rid of the excuses
- Push past your fears

- How to take the necessary actions to achieve your goals

Do you ever wonder why a few people become successes and others don't? The few who become a success are those that do what's needed and do them with consistency. Read this book from **Next Stage Communication** and you will learn the 10 actionable tips to achieving your goals.

Your Powerful
To The Point
Book

How to Overcome
Your Fears and Excuses
to Achieve Your Goals

10 Action Steps to Success

George Gilbert
Award Winning Speaker

Published by **To The Point**
Next Stage Communications
A Subsidiary of Next Stage Speaking

Next Stage Communications
3638 Tioga Way
Las Vegas, NV 89169
(702) 682-8431

ISBN: 9781795434058

I would like to thank my dad for always believing in me and supporting me in everything I ever wanted to do even if I wasn't any good at something, his encouragement gave me the belief that I could succeed. He led by example.

My mother, who helped me make the transition from stand-up comedian to professional speaker by coaching me every day on my presentation skills and keeping me on track by continually reminding me to contact the meeting planners, the event chairs and whoever was in charge of hiring speakers.

Dori Gilbert, who is an example of not giving up under the worst conditions and creating a daily discipline to overcome those challenges.

Al Jensen, who approached me to work together coaching speakers, business executives and entrepreneurs and came up with the idea for creating this book series we are publishing.

Table of Contents

Contents

Introduction

It's a great feeling when you get a speaking gig to get paid to stand up in front of hundreds even thousands of people and share your message. While most people that aspire to be speakers dream about being paid to speak, they underestimate what it takes to get that paid speaking gig.

Simply having the talent isn't enough, in order to get paid to speak you must constantly sell yourself. No one is going to hire you unless you get out and hustle. Just like any profession, to succeed you must be persistent. That's why small business owners and sales people go from networking event to networking event to create relationships and sell their goods and services.

I originally created this book with aspiring speakers in mind but after I started writing it I realized the tools in this book apply to anyone who wants to better themselves and achieve their goals.

The majority of would be speakers fail because they underestimate the amount of work one must put into succeeding. I see speakers who just don't understand that the 45 minutes on the podium is the result of the thousands of hours of work they must put into getting the opportunity to get paid to speak.

When you see a professional speaker like Tony Robins, Super Bowl winning quarterback Tom Brady, or a successful business person like Gary Vaynerchuk, they make it look so easy. The reason they make it look easy is the constant daily routines and thousands of hours they put into preparing and working towards making their goals a reality.

Someone who isn't happy with what they are doing will call it the "daily grind." To those that have a passion for what they do it's not a grind and even when it does get to be a grind they keep going and grind it out because they know they will be a success and happy they didn't quit.

The root of failure is fear. We will create all kinds of excuses to not try because of our fear of failure.

This book is designed to give you action items to help you exam fears that are keeping you from success.

Each action step will help you work to reach your goal. You must figure out how to make the action steps work for you. Once you do you will be on the path to success.

Action Step #1 – Version One is Better Than Version None

My partner Al Jensen and I have a saying, "Version one is better than version none." Too many people never succeed because they are waiting for everything to be perfect. No matter how much you work on it, chances are there is always a better version. Perfectionism stunts success. Even Apple puts their product out to market and as good as it is, once it's been released Apple has to create updates regularly to get the kinks out. You will never know if your speech, product, or service is good until you put it out there. You can't have version two until you've tried version one. You can always go back and improve. Don't let perfectionism stop you from success.

This is especially true with writers. They are always waiting to get another edit done before they release their book until they finally give up on their book.

Perfection is the sin of failure. A sure sign you are going to fail is waiting for everything to be perfect before you take the action of getting your service or product to market. It's better to act and learn from your mistakes than no action at all.

Action Step:

Don't wait to be perfect. What ever it is you are doing go out and do it. You can always improve upon it as you go along.

Action Step #2 - Those that succeed do, those that fail have excuses not to do.

If you want to succeed you have to get rid of the excuses. You can come up with a thousand excuses not to succeed, to not even try. Perfection is just one of those thousands of excuses. Do these excuses sound familiar to you?

- It's bad timing
- I don't have enough time
- I don't have enough money
- My job gets in the way
- I don't have enough education
- I come from a poor family
- No one will take me seriously
- I'm afraid I will fail
- I will start tomorrow
- I don't have all the answers yet
- I don't know the right people
- It's too hard
- Somebody else is already doing it
- I don't know where to begin
- I'm afraid of what my family will say
- I'm afraid of what my friends will say
- I haven't done this before

- It's going to take too long to accomplish
- I'm not that lucky
- I have a disability
- I'll get to it later
- I'm not ready for that level of success
- I have too many things on my plate
- I can't commit until I've seen all the steps
- I can't commit to a schedule
- I tried before and failed
- I'm too tired
- I did everything I could
- I don't have the support system I need
- Big business will just crush me
- I can't think of a niche
- I don't deserve it
- Nobody understands what I am trying to do
- I'm too old
- I'm too young
- Etc. etc. etc.

How many of these excuses have you heard someone use to fail?
How many of these excuses to not get started do you have?
What other excuses do you have to not get started or for failing after your first few attempts?

If you want to fail, you will find an excuse(s) to fail. In fact, if you want to fail you will never run out of excuses to fail.

If you want to succeed you will not let excuses get in your way.

Action Step:

List all your excuses not to try and for failing.
Scratch a line through each excuse.
Rewrite the excuse as an excuse to succeed.

Example: ~~I don't have enough time to do it.~~
I will make time to do it.

Example: ~~I don't have all the answers yet.~~
I will get started and find the answers as I work toward my goal.

Example: ~~I have too many things on my plate~~
I will eliminate the things that distract me from reaching my goal.

Action Step #3 – Stop Being Afraid of Rejection

The fear of rejection is one of the most crippling excuses we have to not even try or to give up too soon. No one likes to be rejected. Whether you are asking someone out on a date, trying for a part in a play, or applying for a job, being rejected can be devasting.

As children playing in a pickup basketball game no one wanted to be the last one picked. Every time the two people picking someone for their team didn't mention my name, I would get more and more anxious until someone picked me. Same thing applies when you get picked over for a job or a position in the company you are applying for. In reality what is the worst thing about not getting picked? Our ego is bruised. I know people who were passed over because they weren't good enough at the time but worked hard and learned from the experience to make themselves worthy of the job. Then when the job opened up again and they were perfect for the job, they opted not to apply out of fear of being rejected again.
If you want to succeed at reaching your goal you must not be afraid of rejection. They would rather stay in the same position rather than try out of fear of rejection.

Even if you don't get the job the worse thing that happens is you stay in the same position.

Action Step:

How to overcome the fear of rejection.

1. **Don't take rejection personally (you don't know why you were rejected. It may not have had anything personally to do with you.)**
2. **The more you try the better the odds are of not getting rejected.**
3. **When you do get rejected try and ask why you weren't chosen.**
4. **Learn from your rejection. If the way you are doing something isn't working, try doing it differently.**

Action Step #4 – Stop Being Afraid of Success

Are you afraid of success? I know this sounds ridiculous, but some people are actually afraid of success because it means they will have to work harder, longer hours, maybe move, get up in front of an audience and speak to people, the list goes on an on. In other words, change even for the reward can be scary because it forces you to get out of your comfort zone and grow.

I have experienced the fear of success. I knew that if I were to be a success as a comedian I would have to travel more. I was comfortable where I was but I had to force myself to get over that fear of success because I really wanted to make a living making people laugh.

Fear of success can also be a fear of failure. You may want a job so bad that you can't stop thinking about it. You know you are qualified. You know you want the pay increase. You know how much better your life will be when you get promoted or the job of your dreams and then your insecurities take over and you start to think but what if I get the job or position and then I fail. I will embarrass myself. I could lose the job I already have. What if I move and I don't like the location once I get settled in.

Action Steps:

When those fears of success start to pop up preventing you from going after what you want:

Write out why you wanted the job, promotion, etc.

Create a list of all the benefits as a result of getting what you want

Create a list of all your negative thoughts of getting what you thought you wanted?

Ask yourself are the positives worth the effort?

If not, then maybe the timing is wrong, or it was just more of a dream than an actual goal.

Action Step #5 - Don't use other people as an excuse not to go after your goals

Your goals are your goals, no one else's and yet we tend to react to other people's opinion of what they think we should not do. Just because someone else can't envision your goal doesn't mean its not worth doing. Everyone has their own filter they see the world through. You are not responsible for their limited thinking. Maybe they tried and failed. Maybe they don't have the education. Maybe deep down they are jealous to see you succeed. Maybe they feel they will lose you if you succeed. Maybe if you succeed that will make them look like a loser.

Just because someone can't envision your success doesn't mean you won't be a success. However, if you listen to the nay sayers you will prove them right. If you try you may also prove them right but who knows, you might just prove them wrong and maybe even give them confidence from leading by example.

If you are prone to giving into people who are negative and can't envision you succeeding just ask yourself are they fulfilling their goals? The person who reaches his/her goals doesn't usually belittle someone else's goals.

Action Steps:

Ask yourself why the people you are sharing your goals with don't think you can succeed.

Quietly stop associating with people who don't believe you can attain your goals and start associating with positive people who will support you in achieving your goals.

Action Step #6 Don't use other people as an excuse for failure

When we fail we want to blame everyone but ourselves. It's easier to put the blame on someone else rather than take a hard look at our self and accept the real reason we failed.

Blaming your family and your upbringing for failing is a surefire way to never trying, let alone succeeding.

Blaming your teacher because he/she said you were too dumb to succeed isn't an excuse for not trying.

Blaming a co-worker because they got the job and you didn't won't lead to you getting the promotion in the future.

You can always find someone to blame and use them as an excuse to fail or you can take a hard honest look at yourself and figure out what it is you need to do the next time to succeed and prove them wrong.

Action Steps:

Next time you start to blame someone for failing take a hard honest look at yourself and ask yourself what did they really do to keep you from your success.

Ask yourself what you could have done to have succeeded regardless of what they may have done to keep you from succeeding.

Action Step #7 – Don't get distracted by busy work

Fear of failure will play many tricks on us. One trick is busy work. We trick ourselves into creating tasks that appear to help toward reaching our goals but, these tasks are not helping us get any closer. You should be concentrating on the most important step you can take to reach your goal.

Many of my colleagues just starting out in the speaking business were challenged by another colleague to take the "90 Day Facebook Live Challenge." Most of them got excited and took the challenge. While it is a good learning experience to get comfortable with the social media platform and the discipline of doing something every day for 90 days, it is busy work if you are trying to become a paid professional public speaker. If you want to speak you have to contact people who can hire you to speak. I suggested they take the "90 Calls to Speak Challenge." I challenged them to call or email at least one person a day who could book them to speak. It's funny the same people who embraced the Facebook Live Challenge had all kind of reasons why that was important, but no one took me up on the challenge that could directly move their career forward. Why? Because deep down they were afraid of getting rejected. They were afraid of failure.

Busy work keeps us thinking we are on the right track and it will lead to success, but the reality is busy work keep us from achieving our goals.

All busy work does is it keeps the dream alive.

Action Steps:

Make a list of everything you are doing to achieve your goal.

Now go through the list line by line and ask yourself is this action the most important task I can do to reach my goal? If it isn't then scratch it off your list of immediate tasks. When you have narrowed your tasks down to just one start implementing that task and you will reach your goal faster.

Action Step #8 – Don't pay to keep the dream alive

I mentioned in the previous chapter that busy work just keeps the dream alive, but it doesn't get you any closer to the goal.

Another way to keep the dream alive is to pay thousands of dollars to go to conferences to help motivate you. You spend a day, a weekend or even a week at one of these conferences. They get you pumped up and excited about your goals. They give you great tools to work with but after you leave the conference and the adrenalin and endorphins wear off for some reason the tools you were given never seem to get utilized. The reason is there really isn't any accountability.

Al and I had a client that spent most of her savings going from one motivational conference to another. The difference between a conference with thousands in the audience and us one-on-one coaching you is that we hold you accountable and expect you to do your homework. The client didn't like that. It became apparent she would rather spend all her money until it ran out keeping the dream alive than working on her goals.

Action Steps:

If you go to a conference, make sure you get your money's worth and use the tools you were given to work towards your goal.

Hire a coach that will hold you accountable and make sure you are working to reach your goal and not just to keep the dream alive.

Action Step #9 – Timing

"There is no tomorrow! There is no tomorrow! There is no Tomorrow! Apollo Creed to Rocky Balboa

You can always blame bad timing on why you haven't started working toward your goal.

Bad timing excuses are:
- It's the economy
- It's an election year
- Nostradamus predicted the end is near

Yes, I am being facetious. If you are afraid of failure you will come up with all kinds of crazy excuses to not get started. Even something as lame as, "I am too tired, I'll start tomorrow", will be an excuse not to work towards your goal because you don't want to face your fear of failure.

Too many, "I'll start tomorrow" excuses end up as an excuse to never get started and before you know it tomorrow has come and gone and your goal has become a faded dream.

Don't let your goals become a faded dream, act now if you are serious about reaching your goal.

Action Steps:

Don't wait to start working towards your goal. Even if the timing isn't perfect, if you are serious about reaching your goal you will make the time to get started.

Getting started is the key to overcoming your fear of failure and to reaching your goal.

Action Step #10 - Take ownership: You are responsible for you, your attitude and your failures

There comes a time when you must stop coming up with excuses to not try, to overcome your failures and take ownership of your life and your circumstances. It is very easy to give up and blame everyone and everything on why you are where you are but if you want to succeed there is only one obstacle in your way.

Excuses are only as legitimate as you let them be.

That obstacle is YOU!

Action Steps:

Get over yourself and don't use excuses to fail or not even try.
Ask yourself, what is really keeping me from reaching my goals?

ABOUT THE AUTHOR

George Gilbert has many years' experience as a professional public speaker, author and executive speech coach. He started out as a stand-up comedian and segued his comedy into motivational humor after using humor to overcome challenges in his personal and professional life. George speaks about the importance of humor in business, the role humor plays in the work place and the benefits of laughter in life. His unique and entertaining presentations emphasize team-building, customer service, and wellness. He gets his message across through fun and humor. George formed Originally Speaking™ to combine his public speaking skills along with his business and writing skills to bring presentations on the importance of humor to businesses and professional organizations.

In 2001, "due to his professionalism and outstanding achievements in public speaking," he was awarded the title of Accredited Speaker, becoming only the 50th person in the world to achieve this designation. George's show business background gives him a commanding stage presence.

George's mission is to provide information and inspiration to corporations and professional organizations by demonstrating, in an entertaining format, how humor can benefit their businesses and lives.

George has written and published:

From Stand-up To Standout – *How to incorporate appropriate humor in to your speeches*

Take Two Laughs and Call Me in the Morning – *Laughter is a wellness program everyone can afford*

Put Their Money Where Your Mouth Is – *Sell yourself as a speaker*

2017: George Gilbert partnered with Al Jensen to form Next Stage Speaking to coach business executives, entrepreneurs, and merging professional speakers on how to improve their speaking skills and sell themselves as a speaker.

2019: George Gilbert and Al Jensen are expanding their services to meet the needs of their clients and are now offering book publishing, webinar training and creation, and how to sell from the back of the room. They have created **Next Stage Communications**

George attributes his success to his parents who led by example, do the best job you can do, love what you do and have fun doing it.

To book George Gilbert to speak to your organization go to:

www.originallyspeaking.com
email George at: george@originallyspeaking.com

To learn more about Next Stage Communications go to: **www.nextstagespeaking.com**

Look for more **To The Point** books